# SUZI, SAM, GEORGE
# & ALICE

For Ann-Marie and Oliver S.G.
For Kate, Rachel and the real George and Alice B.B.

# Suzi, Sam, George & Alice

**Beverley Birch**
**Sally Gardner**

SUZI

SAM

GEORGE

ALICE

Red Fox

Seven o'clock on Sunday morning.
Sleeping time.
Lazy time.

Not for Suzi and Sam and George and Alice.

Time for Suzi to help the sick.
Time for Sam to bound and bounce.
Time for Alice's circus trick.

Time for George to . . .

. . . guard something.

Eight o'clock on Sunday morning.
Getting up and going downstairs time.

Not for Suzi and Sam and George and Alice.

Time for tunnelling deep
and climbing high
and flying through the air.

Time for George to . . .

. . . guard something.

Nine o'clock on Sunday morning.
Breakfast time.
Eating time.
Cereal and toast and honey time.

Not for Suzi and Sam and George and Alice.

Concert time.
Dancing time.

Time for George to . . .

. . . rest.

Ten o'clock on Sunday morning.
Time for a long, quiet chat with Gran.

Not for Suzi and Sam and George and Alice.

Time for brave explorers to camp
in blizzards.
Time for bears to find warm dens.
Time for snow leopards to leap
from icy mountain kingdoms.

Time for George to . . .

. . . guard something.

Eleven o'clock on Sunday morning.
Quiet time.
Sitting in the sun and reading time.

Not for Suzi and Sam and George and Alice.

Time to soar to dizzy heights
and swing across ravines,
to hang from swaying jungle trees.

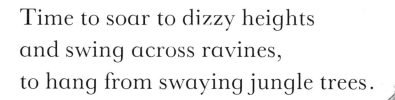

Time for George to . . .

. . . have another rest.

Twelve o'clock on Sunday morning.
Cooking time.
Mixing time.

Not for Suzi and Sam and George and Alice.

Party time.
Playing time.
Time to greet the toys.

Time for George to . . .

. . . guard something.

One o'clock on Sunday afternoon.
Lunch time.
Munch time.

Not for Suzi and Sam and George and Alice.

Time to track the untamed jungle.
Time to find the tiger's trail.

Time for George to . . .

. . . rest.

Two o'clock on Sunday afternoon.
Quiet after lunch time.

Not for Suzi and Sam and George and Alice.

Time for dams and waterfalls
and roaring ocean waves.

Time for George to . . .

. . . keep his feet dry.

Three o'clock on Sunday afternoon.
Running in the park time.
Leaping and jumping and rolling time.

Three o'clock . . .

. . . four o'clock.

Four o'clock!

'It's very quiet!' said Mum.
'Where are Suzi and Sam and George and Alice?'

'SUZI!'

'SAM!'

'GEORGE!'

'ALICE!'

'It's coming out time!'
'It's stopping-this-game-this-minute time!'

'It's SOMETHING-TERRIBLE-HAS-HAPPENED time,'
said Dad.

'Too-quiet time,
Too-empty time.'

On-their-own time!
Out-of-sight time!

TIME
for Suzi and Sam and George and Alice
to do something

truly, truly

TRULY

TERRIBLE!

A Red Fox Book

Published by Random House Children's Books
20 Vauxhall Bridge Road, London SW1V 2SA

A division of Random House UK Ltd
London Melbourne Sydney Auckland
Johannesburg and agencies throughout the world

1 3 5 7 9 10 8 6 4 2

First published in Great Britain by The Bodley Head 1993

Red Fox edition 1994

Printed in Singapore

RANDOM HOUSE UK Limited Reg. No. 954009